NEW BRUNSWICK Pictorial Cookbook

Photographs by Sherman Hines

NIMBUS PUBLISHING LTD

Nimbus Publishing Limited
P.O. Box 9301, Station A
Halifax, Nova Scotia
B3K 5N5

Design: Arthur Carter, Halifax

Recipes compiled by Margaret Jones
Credits: Winsor-Jones family collection, New Brun-
swick Department of Fisheries and Aquaculture,
Kings Landing Historical Settlement, and New
Brunswick Department of Agriculture, Market Devel-
opment Branch

Photograph pp. 34-35 reprinted with permission of
Canadian Living

Canadian Cataloguing-in-Publication Data

Hines, Sherman, 1941-

New Brunswick pictorial cookbook

ISBN 0-921054-61-0

1. Cookery, Canadian— New Brunswick style.
2. New Brunswick— Description and travel— 1981-
—Views.*
I. Title

TX715.6.H56 1991   641.59715'1   C90-097710-8

Printed and bound in Hong Kong,
by Everbest Printing Company, Ltd.

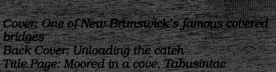

*Cover: One of New Brunswick's famous covered
bridges*
Back Cover: Unloading the catch
Title Page: Moored in a cove, Tabusintac
Table of Contents: Weir fishing, Grand Manan
Introduction: Grazing cattle, Saint John River Valley

Table of Contents

Introduction

*By Margaret Jones
and Pamela Winsor*

Host to some of this country's richest culinary resources, New Brunswick nestles on the Atlantic coast. The waves and winds of the Bay of Fundy and the Baie des Chaleurs bring some of the finest seafood available. The forests, rivers, marshes, and fields offer their own special colours and flavours to add to the Canadian foodbasket.

Since the days of the native peoples and the early French settlers, who arrived in the seventeenth century, man has lived off the bounties of the land and the waters. The English, the United Empire Loyalists, the Irish, and the European immigrants also contributed to the diversity of the culinary culture of New Brunswick.

From the beginning, the province consisted of tiny fishing communities along the rugged coastlines, lumber camps in the wooded interior, and farms along the river valleys. The forests of "the Picture Province" have always been home to deer, moose, and a variety of gamebirds, all of which were staples for the early settlers. Over the years, improved techniques in aquaculture and agriculture have increased the yield of the land and the waters.

Flavourful native ingredients have developed into some time-honoured culinary treats. To enjoy them, one must appreciate the changing seasons and how they determine the cuisine. A springtime tradition and tasty celebration at winter's end is the annual tapping of red and white sugar-maple trees. The sweet sap is boiled until it becomes a concentrated syrup, then served warm on a stack of steaming pancakes or on ice cream. Other sap products are maple butter, cream, and taffy.

Another natural delicacy is the fiddlehead, a young ostrich fern named for its resemblance to a fiddle. Most of the annual fiddlehead crop is gathered by Malecite Indians and sold in grocery stores and at farmers' markets in early spring. This green vegetable is often served as a side dish with fish or meat. If allowed to mature, fiddleheads grow into graceful ferns along the riverbanks.

Summer makes only a brief appearance in New Brunswick. The length of the show, however, is not indicative of the calibre of the act. While some people go on holiday, many toil long hours to make the most of the short growing season. Orchards in the Keswick Valley are tended to ensure the finest of apple crops,

while potato fields in western New Brunswick are tilled expertly until early fall. Seed potatoes are shipped worldwide— just one of the province's first-class products.

Wild and cultivated berries are popular ingredients. They are wonderful fresh or in a variety of baked and preserved goods. Cranberries, blueberries, and strawberries flourish in New Brunswick, and for generations, it has been a family tradition to "go picking."

One natural sea vegetable is dulse, which is harvested in summer on the coast of Grand Manan. It is a delicious, nutritious snack food, and it can be flaked or shredded and added to chowders, omelettes, or breads. Also from the ocean, the lobster is among the tastiest in the world. As well, the bays and rivers yield herring, smelts, trout, salmon, haddock, halibut, and shad. Not to be forgotten are clams, mussels, quahogs, scallops, crab, and shrimp. No Maritime summer holiday would be complete without a clam bake or a lobster boil on the beach.

When summer comes to a close, the autumn hillsides glow with the "scarlet of the maples" and yellow of the poplars. The native poet Bliss Carman once wrote, "There is something in the autumn that is nature to my blood...." Certainly, the splendour of the leaves is a backdrop to the hum of activity in the potato fields and the apple orchards. In the kitchens, the aroma of pickle-making tells where the onions, cucumbers, tomatoes, and beets have been stored.

The chill of the fall breeze, however, serves as a warning. Frost and snow will follow as surely as night follows day. Before long, the days are shorter, the fields are blanketed in white, snowplows are working overtime, and warm fires are aglow. New Brunswickers, undaunted by nature's frosty glare, turn frozen lakes and streams into skating rinks and ice-fishing spots. Then they go home to a wonderful supper of fried smelts, baked potatoes, pickled beets, and hot apple crisp.

The beauty and bounty of New Brunswick are inseparable. Through his lens, Sherman Hines has captured both the fleeting moments of light and the stark enduring images that form the contrasts of the province. The kitchens provide for the palate what the photographs provide for the eye. Combine and simmer gently for hours.

Natives of rural New Brunswick, Margaret Jones and Pamela Winsor have long been interested in the history of the province and its traditional cuisine.

Light Lobster Dip

1 cup (250 mL) lobster meat
1 cup (250 mL) 2% cottage cheese
2 tbsp (25 mL) light mayonnaise
1 tsp (5 mL) lemon juice
1 to 2 tbsp (15 to 25 mL) finely
*   chopped green onion*
1/2 garlic clove, minced
2 drops Tabasco sauce
1/2 tsp (2 mL) salt
Pepper to taste

Drain lobster and remove cartilage.
Cut into small pieces and set aside.
Purée cottage cheese and mix with
remaining ingredients. Stir in
lobster meat and chill dip for several
hours. Serve with crackers or fresh
vegetables.

Photo: Swallowtail Light at sunset,
Grand Manan

Cranberry Salad

*Juice of 1 orange, plus water to make
   1-1/2 cups (375 mL)
1 pkg lemon jelly powder
3/4 cup (175 mL) sugar
Rind of 1 orange
2 cups (500 mL) chopped cranberries
3/4 cup (175 mL) diced celery*

Heat orange juice and water. Add
jelly powder and sugar, stirring until
dissolved. Let mixture cool until
partly set. Add orange rind, cranberries, and celery. Pour into a mould
and place in refrigerator.

Waldorf Salad Supreme

4 Cortland apples, cored and cubed
1 tbsp (15 mL) lemon juice
1 cup (250 mL) sliced celery
1/2 cup (125 mL) chopped dates
2/3 cup (150 mL) plain yogurt
Crisp lettuce leaves

Combine apples and lemon juice, tossing well. Add celery and dates. Add yogurt, stirring well to coat celery and fruit. Serve on lettuce leaves. Serves 4.

Note: If desired, substitute 1/3 cup (75 mL) sour cream and 1/3 cup (75 mL) mayonnaise for yogurt.

Photo: Saint John Market

Young fern fronds, fiddleheads are picked along the riverbanks just after the spring freshet. Only the tops are eaten, and they must be rinsed several times to remove the brown scale.

Cream of Mussels and Fiddleheads

1 lb (500 g) fresh mussels
2 green onions, chopped
1 cup (250 mL) chopped onion
1/4 cup (50 mL) butter
1 cup (250 mL) dry white wine
1 cup (250 mL) water
1/4 tsp (1 mL) thyme
1/4 tsp (1 mL) chopped parsley
1/4 cup (50 mL) chopped onion
1 tbsp (15 mL) butter
1 cup (250 mL) cooked fiddleheads
Pinch nutmeg
Salt and pepper to taste
1 egg yolk
1/2 cup (125 mL) whipping cream
Crisp bacon pieces for garnish
  (optional)
Sour cream for garnish (optional)

Scrub and thoroughly wash mussels, discarding dead ones. Remove byssus threads. Sauté green onions and 1 cup (250 mL) chopped onion in 1/4 cup (50 mL) butter until tender. Add wine, water, thyme, and parsley. Bring to a boil. Add mussels, cover, and steam on high heat until shells open, about 5 minutes. Strain mussel broth through several layers of cheesecloth and reserve 5 cups (1.25 L). Remove mussels from shells and set aside. Sauté 1/4 cup (50 mL) onion in 1 tbsp (15 mL) butter until transparent. Stir in fiddleheads, nutmeg, salt, and pepper. Purée mixture and place in a saucepan. Add reserved broth. Whisk together egg yolk and cream and gradually add to fiddlehead mixture. Add mussels and heat through. Garnish soup with bacon pieces and sour cream. Serves 4.

Left: Sawmill, Kings Landing Historical Settlement
Right: Saint John

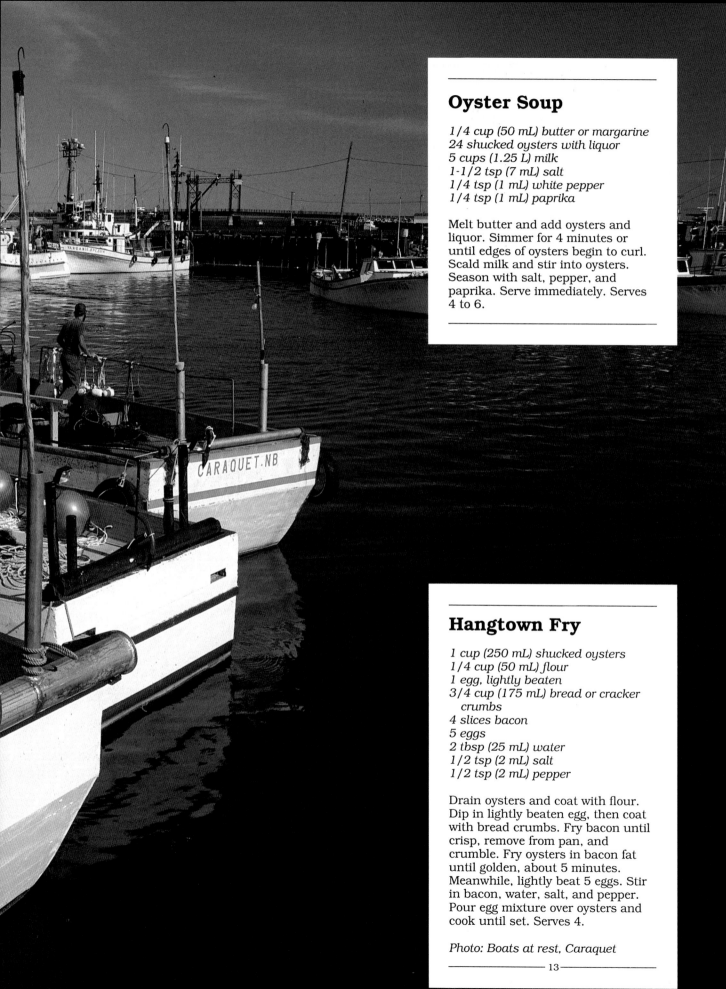

Oyster Soup

1/4 cup (50 mL) butter or margarine
24 shucked oysters with liquor
5 cups (1.25 L) milk
1-1/2 tsp (7 mL) salt
1/4 tsp (1 mL) white pepper
1/4 tsp (1 mL) paprika

Melt butter and add oysters and liquor. Simmer for 4 minutes or until edges of oysters begin to curl. Scald milk and stir into oysters. Season with salt, pepper, and paprika. Serve immediately. Serves 4 to 6.

Hangtown Fry

1 cup (250 mL) shucked oysters
1/4 cup (50 mL) flour
1 egg, lightly beaten
3/4 cup (175 mL) bread or cracker
  crumbs
4 slices bacon
5 eggs
2 tbsp (25 mL) water
1/2 tsp (2 mL) salt
1/2 tsp (2 mL) pepper

Drain oysters and coat with flour. Dip in lightly beaten egg, then coat with bread crumbs. Fry bacon until crisp, remove from pan, and crumble. Fry oysters in bacon fat until golden, about 5 minutes. Meanwhile, lightly beat 5 eggs. Stir in bacon, water, salt, and pepper. Pour egg mixture over oysters and cook until set. Serves 4.

Photo: Boats at rest, Caraquet

Hoppel Poppel

4 potatoes, thinly sliced
6 strips bacon, diced
1 onion, finely chopped
1/2 cup (125 mL) chopped
    mushrooms
4 large eggs
1 tsp (5 mL) salt
1/2 tsp (2 mL) pepper
1/2 cup (125 mL) grated Cheddar
    cheese
1 tbsp (15 mL) chopped fresh parsley
1 tsp (5 mL) caraway seeds

Cook potatoes in a small amount of
water. Meanwhile, fry together
bacon, onion, and mushrooms until
tender. Drain potatoes and add to
bacon mixture, mixing well. Heat
through. Beat eggs with salt and
pepper and pour over potato mixture but do not stir. Sprinkle with
cheese, parsley, and caraway seeds.
Cover and cook at very low heat
until eggs set. Brown under broiler.
Serves 4.

*Photo: Horses grazing on a valley
farm*

15

Chicken Croquettes

1-3/4 cups (425 mL) chopped,
  cooked chicken
1/2 tsp (2 mL) salt
1/4 tsp (1 mL) celery salt
Few grains pepper
1 tsp (5 mL) lemon juice
Few drops onion juice
1 tsp (5 mL) chopped parsley
1 cup (250 mL) white sauce
1 egg, beaten
Fine bread crumbs
White sauce:
3 tbsp (50 mL) butter
3 tbsp (50 mL) flour

1 cup (250 mL) milk
1/4 tsp (1 mL) salt
1/8 tsp (1 mL) pepper

Prepare white sauce. In a double
boiler, melt butter and stir in flour.
Gradually add milk, stirring constantly until thick. Season with
1/4 tsp (1 mL) salt and pepper.

Prepare croquettes. Mix together all
ingredients except beaten egg and
bread crumbs. Form into egg-size
balls. Dip each ball in beaten egg,
coating completely, and roll in
bread crumbs. Fry in deep fat for 5
minutes.

16

Potato Croquettes

2 cups (500 mL) hot riced potatoes
2 tbsp (25 mL) butter
1/2 tsp (2 mL) salt
1/8 tsp (1 mL) pepper
1/4 tsp (1 mL) celery salt
Few drops onion juice
1 egg yolk
1 tsp (5 mL) chopped parsley
1 egg, beaten
Fine bread crumbs

Mix together all ingredients except
beaten egg and bread crumbs; form
into medium-size balls. Dip each
ball in beaten egg, coating completely, and roll in bread crumbs.
Fry in deep fat for 5 minutes.

*Photo: Potato fields near
Edmundston*

17

Cipate du Restigouche

1 lb (500 g) beef
1 lb (500 g) pork
1 lb (500 g) chicken or turkey
1 lb (500 g) venison
1 lb (500 g) moose meat
1 rabbit
Partridge breast
3 medium-size onions, finely chopped
1 tbsp (15 mL) mixed spices to taste
Salt and pepper to taste
1/2 lb (250 g) salt pork, thinly sliced
7 to 9 lb (3.5 to 4.5 kg) potatoes,
  peeled and cubed
Stock from bones
Dough:
2 cups (500 mL) flour
3/4 cup (175 mL) lukewarm stock
  from bones
Pinch salt

Bone meat and cut into 1/2-inch
(1-cm) cubes. Make stock with

bones and set aside 3/4 cup (175 mL) for dough. Mix together meat, onions, spices, salt, and pepper; refrigerate for 1 hour.

Prepare dough. Mix together flour, 3/4 cup (175 mL) stock, and pinch of salt. Roll out and cut half of dough into 1-inch (2.5-cm) squares. Set aside other half of dough to cover *cipate*.

In 1 or 2 large pots, combine salt pork, potatoes, meat mixture, squares of dough, and stock, mixing well. Cover with remaining pastry. Refrigerate for a few hours or until stock is at same level as pastry. Add more stock or water if necessary. Bake in a 375°F (190°C) oven for 1 hour. Reduce temperature to 250°F (130°C) and bake for 4 to 5 more hours. Serves 15 to 18.

Left: Wharf at Tabusintac
Right: Logging at Grand Falls

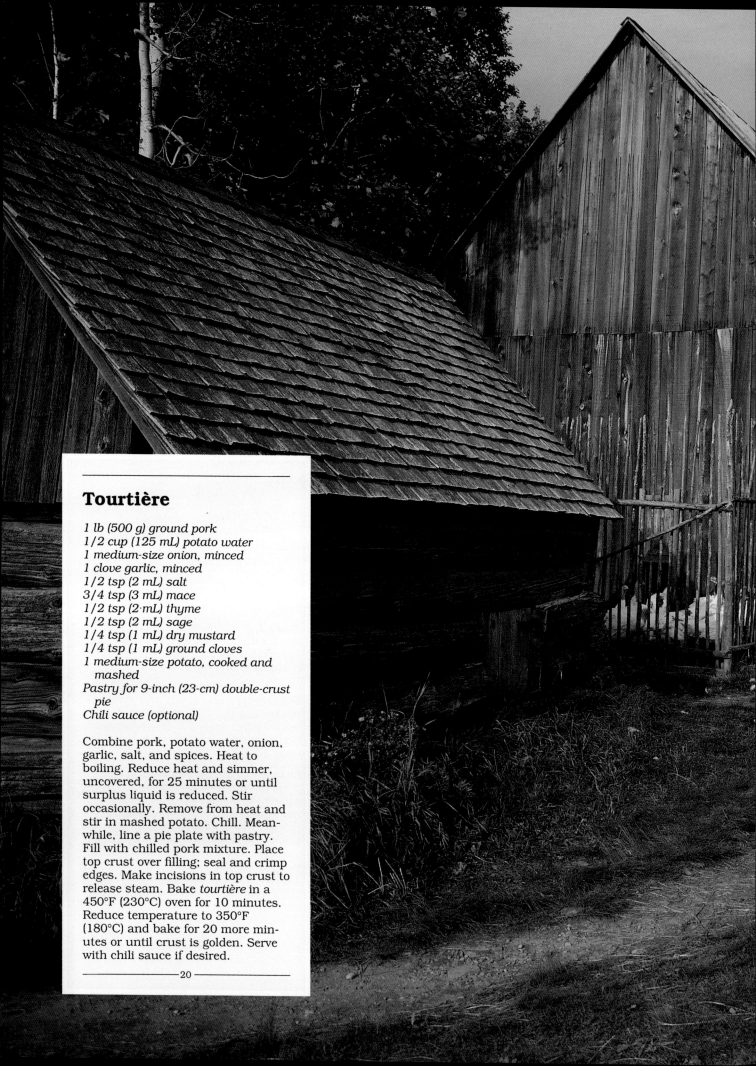

Tourtière

1 lb (500 g) ground pork
1/2 cup (125 mL) potato water
1 medium-size onion, minced
1 clove garlic, minced
1/2 tsp (2 mL) salt
3/4 tsp (3 mL) mace
1/2 tsp (2·mL) thyme
1/2 tsp (2 mL) sage
1/4 tsp (1 mL) dry mustard
1/4 tsp (1 mL) ground cloves
1 medium-size potato, cooked and
*   mashed*
Pastry for 9-inch (23-cm) double-crust
*   pie*
Chili sauce (optional)

Combine pork, potato water, onion, garlic, salt, and spices. Heat to boiling. Reduce heat and simmer, uncovered, for 25 minutes or until surplus liquid is reduced. Stir occasionally. Remove from heat and stir in mashed potato. Chill. Meanwhile, line a pie plate with pastry. Fill with chilled pork mixture. Place top crust over filling; seal and crimp edges. Make incisions in top crust to release steam. Bake *tourtière* in a 450°F (230°C) oven for 10 minutes. Reduce temperature to 350°F (180°C) and bake for 20 more minutes or until crust is golden. Serve with chili sauce if desired.

Poutines Rapées

1/2 lb (250 g) salt pork, diced
30 medium-size potatoes
Salt and pepper to taste
1/2 lb (250 g) ground pork
Flour

Soak salt pork in cold water. Meanwhile, boil 10 potatoes, drain, and mash. Grate remaining 20 potatoes and squeeze excess liquid through cheesecloth. (Make sure grated potatoes and mashed potatoes are of same consistency.) Mix together mashed and grated potatoes and add salt and pepper. Form snowballs with potato mixture and make a hole in centre of each. Drain salt pork and mix with ground pork. Place 1 tbsp (15 mL) meat mixture in hole in each potato ball, then close opening. Lightly sprinkle each *poutine* with flour and wrap in a piece of cheesecloth. Carefully place 2 or 3 *poutines* at a time in a pot of salted boiling water. Simmer for 2 to 3 hours, making sure that water is always bubbling. Makes about 12 *poutines*.

Note: If desired, substitute 1 1b (500 g) salt pork for mixture of salt pork and ground pork.

Photo: Acadian Historical Village, Caraquet

21

Lobster Thermidor

2 cooked lobsters
2 tbsp (25 mL) margarine
1 cup (250 mL) chopped mushrooms
3 tbsp (50 mL) flour
Dash salt, dry mustard, and paprika
1-1/2 cups (375 mL) milk
1/4 cup (50 mL) grated Cheddar
  cheese
1 tbsp (15 mL) lemon juice
2 tbsp (25 mL) Parmesan cheese

Cut each lobster in half lengthwise.
Remove meat from body and claws,
cut into small pieces, and set aside;
save shells for stuffing. Melt margarine, add mushrooms, and cook
until tender. Blend in flour, salt, dry
mustard, and paprika. Gradually
add milk, stirring until thick and
smooth. Add Cheddar cheese,
stirring until melted. Add lobster
meat and lemon juice, mixing well.
Spoon mixture into lobster shells,
sprinkle with Parmesan cheese, and
broil until lightly browned. Serves 4.

*Photo: Swallowtail Light, Grand
Manan*

22

Prepare this the day before, and take it on a picnic.

Premier's Pie

2 cups (500 mL) rainbow trout
1 cup (250 mL) diced carrots
1 cup (250 mL) diced potatoes
1/2 cup (125 mL) chopped onion
2 garlic cloves, minced
1/4 cup (50 mL) butter or margarine
1/4 cup (50 mL) flour
2 cups (500 mL) milk
1 cup (250 mL) grated mozzarella cheese
2 tsp (10 mL) chopped parsley
1 tsp (5 mL) salt and paprika
1/2 tsp (2 mL) pepper and thyme
1/4 tsp (1 mL) dry mustard
Pastry for 9-inch (23-cm) double-crust pie

Cut trout into small strips, discard skin and bones, and measure flesh. Cook carrots and potatoes; set aside. Sauté onion and garlic in butter until tender. Blend in flour. Cook for 3 minutes, stirring constantly. Meanwhile, scald milk, then add gradually to roux, stirring constantly until thick. Add cheese, parsley, and spices, stirring until cheese melts. Add trout, carrots, and potatoes. Line a pie plate with pastry and fill with trout mixture. Cover with top crust and make incisions to release steam. Bake in a 450°F (230°C) oven for 15 minutes. Reduce temperature to 350°F (180°C) and bake for 30 more minutes. Serves 6.
Photo: Legislative Building, Fredericton

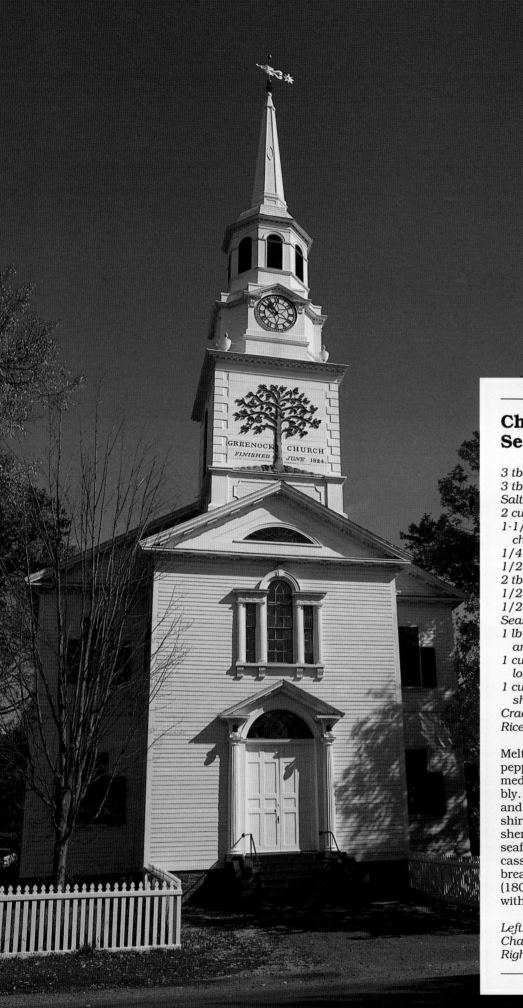

Charlotte County Seafood Casserole

3 tbsp (50 mL) butter
3 tbsp (50 mL) flour
Salt and pepper to taste
2 cups (500 mL) warm whole milk
1-1/2 cups (375 mL) nippy Cheddar
   cheese
1/4 tsp (1 mL) paprika
1/2 tsp (2 mL) Worcestershire sauce
2 tbsp (25 mL) lemon juice
1/2 onion, grated
1/2 cup (125 mL) sherry
Seasoning to taste
1 lb (500 g) haddock fillets, cooked
   and cut into bite-size pieces
1 cup (250 mL) cooked, chopped
   lobster meat
1 cup (250 mL) cooked, shelled
   shrimp
Cracker or bread crumbs
Rice

Melt butter. Blend in flour, salt, and pepper. Stir in milk and cook over medium heat until thick and bubbly. Remove from heat, add cheese and paprika; stir. Add Worcestershire sauce, lemon juice, onion, and sherry. Season to taste. Combine seafood and add to sauce. Place in a casserole and top with cracker or bread crumbs. Bake in a 350°F (180°C) oven for 25 minutes. Serve with rice. Serves 6 to 8.

Left: Greenock Church, St. Andrews, Charlotte County
Right: North Head, Grand Manan

Poached Salmon
with Egg Sauce

3- to 4-lb (1.5- to 2-kg) salmon
1 tsp (5 mL) salt
1/2 cup (125 mL) salt-pork scraps
Water
Egg sauce:
2 tbsp (25 mL) butter
2 tbsp (25 mL) flour
1/2 tsp (2 mL) salt
1/8 tsp (1 mL) pepper
1 cup (250 mL) warm whole milk
2 hard-boiled eggs, chopped

Wipe salmon with a damp cloth.
Wrap in 2 folds of cheesecloth, draw
into a bag, and tie with string.
Combine salt, salt-pork scraps, and
water. Add salmon and simmer
gently, allowing 15 minutes for each
inch (2.5 cm) fish.

Prepare egg sauce. In a double
boiler, melt butter and add flour,
salt, and pepper, stirring constantly
until smooth and bubbly. Add warm
milk, stirring constantly until thick.
Add chopped eggs and cook for 3
more minutes. Serve over poached
salmon.

*Photo: Moored on the Kennebecasis
River*

Oysters Beaverbrook

36 oysters
1 clove garlic, minced
2 tbsp (25 mL) butter
6 scallop shells
1-1/2 cups (375 mL) cooked
    fiddleheads
Sauce:
1 tbsp (15 mL) butter
1 tbsp (15 mL) flour
1/2 cup (125 mL) oyster liquor
1/3 cup (75 mL) grated Swiss cheese
Parmesan cheese

Shuck oysters and drain, reserving liquor. Sauté garlic in 2 tbsp (25 mL) butter. Add oysters and cook until sides curl. Remove oysters from heat, divide equally among scallop shells, and surround with fiddleheads.

Prepare sauce. Melt 1 tbsp (15 mL) butter and blend in flour. Gradually add oyster liquor, stirring constantly until thick. Add Swiss cheese, stirring until melted. Pour sauce over oysters and fiddleheads. Sprinkle with Parmesan cheese and broil until golden. Serves 6.

Left: Leopard, by Jonathan Kenworthy, Beaverbrook Art Gallery, Fredericton
Right: Christ Church Cathedral, Fredericton

Acadian Fish Pancakes

1 lb (500 g) cod fillets
3 eggs, beaten
2 cups (500 mL) finely grated raw
potatoes
2 tbsp (25 mL) flour
2 tbsp (25 mL) finely chopped onion
1 tbsp (15 mL) chopped parsley
1 tsp (5 mL) salt
1/4 tsp (1 mL) nutmeg
1/4 tsp (1 mL) pepper
1/4 cup (50 mL) butter
Applesauce

Skin and finely chop fillets. Mix
together eggs, potatoes, flour, onion,
parsley, salt, nutmeg, and pepper.
Stir in chopped fillets. Melt butter.
Drop cod mixture in 1/3-cup (75-
mL) portions into frying pan and
flatten slightly. Fry for 3 to 4 minutes or until browned. Turn over
carefully and fry for 4 more minutes.
Drain on absorbent paper. Serve
with applesauce. Serves 6.

Fried Smelts

1-1/2 tsp (7 mL) salt
1/4 tsp (1 mL) pepper
1/2 cup (125 mL) flour
1/4 cup (50 mL) cornmeal
Vegetable oil
2 lb (1 kg) cleaned smelts
1/4 cup (50 mL) milk
6 lemon wedges

Mix together salt, pepper, flour, and cornmeal. Heat vegetable oil, about 1/4 inch (1 cm) deep. Dip smelts into milk, then into flour mixture, coating completely. Fry in hot oil for 4 to 5 minutes. Serve hot with lemon wedges. Serves 6.

Photo: A good catch, Tabusintac

31

Fundy Shore Casserole

3 3-1/4-oz (80-g) cans sardines
2 tbsp (25 mL) butter or other fat
2 tbsp (25 mL) chopped onion
2 tbsp (25 mL) flour
1 tsp (5 mL) salt
Dash pepper
2 cups (500 mL) milk
1 cup (250 mL) grated Cheddar
    cheese
2 tsp (10 mL) Worcestershire sauce
5 cups (1.25 L) sliced, cooked
    potatoes

Drain sardines and cut into bite-size
pieces, reserving 6 whole sardines
for garnish. Melt butter and add
onion, cooking until tender but not
brown. Blend in flour, salt, and
pepper. Gradually add milk and
cook until smooth and thick, stirring constantly. Add cheese and
Worcestershire sauce, stirring until
cheese melts. Place half of potatoes
on bottom of a well-greased 2-qt
(2-L) casserole. Arrange sardine
pieces on top, then cover with
remaining potatoes. Cover with
cheese sauce and garnish with
whole sardines. Bake in a 350°F
(180°C) oven for 25 to 30 minutes or
until heated through. Serves 6.

Photo: Rock formation, Fundy Shore

Squash with Walnuts and Maple Syrup

2 winter squash
Salt and freshly ground pepper to
taste
1/3 cup (75 mL) chopped walnuts
1/4 cup (50 mL) butter, melted
1/4 cup (50 mL) maple syrup
1/4 tsp (1 mL) salt
1/4 tsp (1 mL) cinnamon

Cut squash in half lengthwise and remove seeds. Place cut side down in a shallow baking dish and bake in a 350°F (180°C) oven for 35 minutes. Turn squash over and season with salt and pepper. Combine walnuts, butter, maple syrup, 1/4 tsp (1 mL) salt, and cinnamon; spoon into cavities of squash. Bake for 15 more minutes. Serves 4.
Photo: New Brunswick Museum, Saint John

Homemade Custard Ice Cream

2 cups (500 mL) whole milk
1 tbsp (15 mL) flour or cornstarch
3/4 cup (175 mL) sugar
2 egg yolks, lightly beaten
2 cups (500 mL) heavy cream
1/4 tsp (1 mL) salt
1 tbsp (15 mL) vanilla

Scald 1-1/2 cups (375 mL) milk. In a double boiler, combine flour and sugar and add 1/2 cup (125 mL) cold milk. Slowly add scalded milk, stirring constantly. Stir and cook for 8 minutes. Add egg yolks and cook for 2 more minutes. Remove from heat and let cool. Add cream, salt, and vanilla. Place in a 2-qt (2-L) freezer.

36

New Brunswick Maple-Pecan Pie

9-inch (23-cm) pie shell
1/4 cup (50 mL) butter
1 cup (250 mL) packed brown sugar
3 eggs
1/2 cup (125 mL) maple syrup
1-1/2 cups (375 mL) chopped pecans
1 tsp (5 mL) vanilla
1/2 tsp (2 mL) salt
Whipped cream for garnish

Bake pie shell in a 450°F (230°C) oven for 5 to 7 minutes. Remove from oven, cool, and reduce temperature to 375°F (190°C). Cream together butter and brown sugar. Beat in eggs one at a time. Stir in maple syrup, pecans, vanilla, and salt. Pour into pie shell and bake for 40 minutes or until knife inserted in centre comes out clean. Serve warm or cold with whipped cream.

Note: You can also use this recipe to make tarts.

Photo: Tantramar Marsh

Gingerbread with Lemon Sauce

1-3/4 cups (425 mL) flour
1/2 tsp (2 mL) cinnamon
1/2 tsp (2 mL) ground cloves
1 tsp (5 mL) ground ginger
1 tsp (5 mL) baking soda
1/2 tsp (2 mL) salt
1/2 cup (125 mL) boiling water
1 cup (250 mL) molasses
1/2 cup (125 mL) shortening
1 egg
Lemon sauce:
2 tbsp (25 mL) cornstarch
1 cup (250 mL) sugar
Few grains salt
2 tsp (10 mL) grated lemon rind
2 cups (500 mL) water
1/2 cup (125 mL) lemon juice
1 tbsp (15 mL) butter

Prepare gingerbread. Sift together dry ingredients. Add boiling water to molasses. Combine mixtures. Add shortening and egg, beating vigorously. Pour into a greased 8-inch x 8-inch (20-cm x 20-cm) pan and bake in a 350°F (180°C) oven for 1 hour.

Prepare lemon sauce. Mix together cornstarch, sugar, and salt. Add lemon rind. Gradually stir in water and bring to boiling point. Cook and stir until thick, about 5 minutes. Remove from heat and add lemon juice and butter. Serve warm over gingerbread.

Photo: Horses and wagon, Kings Landing Historical Settlement

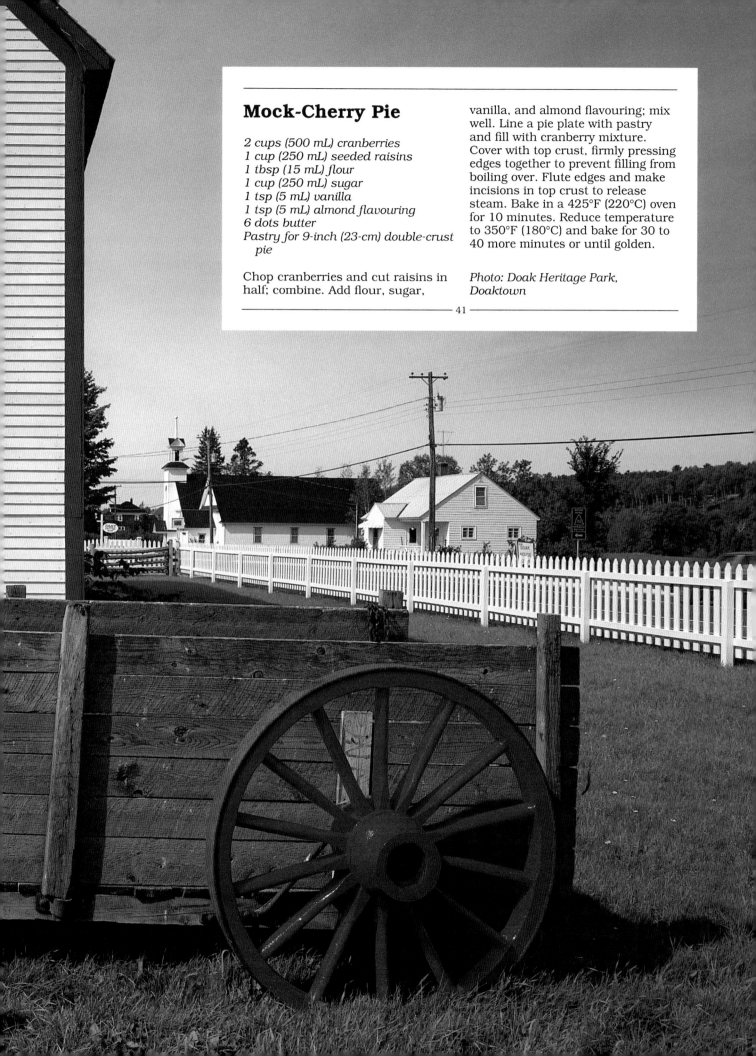

Mock-Cherry Pie

2 cups (500 mL) cranberries
1 cup (250 mL) seeded raisins
1 tbsp (15 mL) flour
1 cup (250 mL) sugar
1 tsp (5 mL) vanilla
1 tsp (5 mL) almond flavouring
6 dots butter
Pastry for 9-inch (23-cm) double-crust
    pie

Chop cranberries and cut raisins in half; combine. Add flour, sugar, vanilla, and almond flavouring; mix well. Line a pie plate with pastry and fill with cranberry mixture. Cover with top crust, firmly pressing edges together to prevent filling from boiling over. Flute edges and make incisions in top crust to release steam. Bake in a 425°F (220°C) oven for 10 minutes. Reduce temperature to 350°F (180°C) and bake for 30 to 40 more minutes or until golden.

Photo: Doak Heritage Park, Doaktown

41

Maple-Custard Parfait

4 eggs, separated
1 cup (500 mL) hot maple syrup
1/8 tsp (1 mL) salt
1 pt (500 mL) whipping cream

Lightly beat egg yolks and slowly
add maple syrup. Add salt. Cook
until thick, then chill. Whip cream
until soft peaks form and fold into
chilled mixture. Beat egg whites
until stiff and fold into cream mixture. Freeze until firm. Makes about
1-1/2 qt (1.5 L).

Left: Horseback riding
Right: University of New Brunswick,
Fredericton

Coddled Rhubarb

4 cups (1 L) chopped rhubarb
1 cup (250 mL) sugar
1/2 cup (125 mL) boiling water

Remove leaf and stem ends of
rhubarb. Chop into 1-inch (2.5-cm)
pieces, removing strings when
necessary. Wash and measure. In a
double boiler, mix together sugar,
rhubarb, and boiling water. Cook
only until fruit is tender, using a
fork for stirring. Chill before serving.

———— 44 ————

Keswick Apple Crisp

4 cups (1 L) sliced, pared, and cored
  baking apples
2/3 to 3/4 cup (150 to 175 mL)
  packed brown sugar
1/2 cup (125 mL) flour
1/2 cup (125 mL) rolled oats
3/4 tsp (3 mL) cinnamon
3/4 tsp (3 mL) nutmeg
1/3 cup (75 mL) soft butter
Cream or ice cream

Place apples in a greased 8-inch x
8-inch (20-cm x 20-cm) baking dish.
Blend together remaining ingredients until mixture is crumbly.
Spread over apples. Bake in a 375°F
(190°C) oven for 30 to 35 minutes or
until apples are tender and topping
is golden. Serve with cream or ice
cream. Serves 6 to 8.

*Photo: Snaking rail fence and grove
of fruit trees*

New Brunswick Maple-Syrup Cheesecake

Crust:
5 oz (150 g) graham-wafer crumbs
1/4 cup (50 mL) butter, melted
2 tbsp (25 mL) maple syrup

Filling:
1-1/2 cups (375 mL) maple syrup
3 eggs
1-1/2 lb (750 g) cream cheese, softened
2 tbsp (25 mL) flour
1/2 tsp (2 mL) vanilla

Garnish:
1 cup (250 mL) whipping cream
1/3 cup (75 mL) chopped almonds, toasted
1 cup (250 mL) chocolate curls

Prepare crust. Combine graham-wafer crumbs, butter, and 2 tbsp (25 mL) maple syrup, mixing well. Press into bottom of a 9-inch (2.5-L) springform pan. Bake in a 325°F (160°C) oven for 10 minutes or until golden. Let cool.

Prepare filling. Boil 1-1/2 cups (375 mL) maple syrup over medium to high heat for 5 to 10 minutes without stirring, until syrup reaches softball stage or candy thermometer registers 234°F (112°C). Remove from heat and let bubbles subside. Syrup should be reduced by half. Lightly beat eggs and gradually add syrup, beating at medium speed for 5 to 10 minutes. Increase to high speed and beat until thick. Let cool. Beat cream cheese until light and fluffy. Beat in flour. Gradually beat in maple-syrup mixture and vanilla. Pour filling into springform pan. Bake in a 425°F (220°C) oven for 10 minutes. Reduce temperature to 250°F (130°C) and bake for 45 to 55 more minutes or until centre is firm to touch. Run knife around edge of pan. Cool completely, remove side of pan, and chill well.

Prepare garnish. Whip cream. Using a pastry bag, pipe cream around edge of cake. Sprinkle with almonds. Sprinkle sides and top of cheesecake with chocolate curls. Serves 10 to 12.

Photo: Marshlands Inn, Sackville

Hot-Milk Cake

2 eggs
1 cup (250 mL) sugar
1 tbsp (15 mL) butter
1 cup (250 mL) flour
1 tsp (5 mL) baking powder
1/2 tsp (2 mL) salt
1/2 cup (125 mL) hot milk
3/4 tsp (3 mL) lemon flavouring
Crushed strawberries
Cream

Beat eggs well. Add sugar and butter. Sift together flour, baking powder, and salt. Add to egg mixture. Beat in hot milk and lemon flavouring. Pour into a greased 8-inch x 8-inch (20-cm x 20-cm) pan and bake in a 350°F (180°C) oven for 25 minutes. Serve with crushed strawberries and cream.

Photo: Holsteins and dandelions, Saint John River Valley

48

Plum Pudding

2 cups (500 mL) currants
3 cups (750 mL) raisins
4 large apples, chopped
1-1/2 cups (375 mL) flour
2 cups (500 mL) suet or 1-1/2 cups
    (375 mL) butter
1 cup (250 mL) sugar
4 eggs
1/2 cup (125 mL) molasses
1 tsp (5 mL) baking soda
2 cups (500 mL) bread crumbs
Salt to taste
Cloves, allspice, and cinnamon to
    taste

Combine currants, raisins, and apples and sprinkle with a small portion of flour. Cream together suet and sugar. Add eggs one at a time. Combine molasses and baking soda and add to egg mixture. Stir in remaining flour, bread crumbs, fruit, salt, and spices. Line tins with brown paper and grease with shortening. Place pudding in tins, cover with wax paper, and secure with string. Steam for 4 hours.

Photo: Winter scene, Havelock

51

Belleisle Wild-Blueberry Buckle

4 tbsp (60 mL) shortening
1/2 cup (125 mL) brown sugar
1 egg
1 cup (250 mL) flour
1-1/2 tsp (7 mL) baking powder
1/4 tsp (1 mL) salt
1/3 cup (75 mL) milk
2 cups (500 mL) wild blueberries
Whipped cream or ice cream

Topping:
1/3 cup (75 mL) brown sugar
1/3 cup (75 mL) flour
2 tbsp (25 mL) butter

Cream together shortening and
1/2 cup (125 mL) brown sugar. Beat
in egg. Combine 1 cup (250 mL)
flour, baking powder, and salt. Add
to shortening mixture alternately
with milk. Spread in a greased
9-inch x 9-inch (23-cm x 23-cm)
baking pan. Cover with blueberries.

Prepare topping. Combine 1/3 cup
(75 mL) brown sugar and 1/3 cup
(75 mL) flour. Cut in butter until
mixture resembles coarse crumbs.
Sprinkle over blueberries. Bake in a
350°F (180°C) oven for 40 to 45
minutes or until golden. Serve with
whipped cream or ice cream if
desired.

Left: Tray of blueberries
Right: Covered bridge near Sackville

Strawberry Tea Bread

2 cups (500 mL) flour
1-1/2 cups (375 mL) quick-cooking
   rolled oats
1 tsp (5 mL) cinnamon
1 tsp (5 mL) salt
1 tsp (5 mL) baking soda
1/2 tsp (2 mL) baking powder
3 eggs
1 cup (250 mL) sugar
1 cup (250 mL) vegetable oil
1 tsp (5 mL) vanilla
2 cups (500 mL) crushed
   strawberries

Mix together flour, rolled oats,
cinnamon, salt, baking soda, and
baking powder. Beat together eggs,
sugar, vegetable oil, and vanilla. Stir
in dry ingredients just until well
mixed. Add crushed strawberries,
stirring to combine completely. Pour
batter into 2 greased and floured
8-inch x 4-inch (20-cm x 10-cm) loaf
pans. Bake in a 375°F (190°C) oven
for 45 to 50 minutes or until tops
are brown, firm to touch, and a
knife inserted in centre comes out
clean. Run knife around edges of
loaf pans and let bread cool in pans
for 10 minutes. Turn onto a wire
rack and let cool completely.

*Left: Rich wood, leaded glass, and
silver*
Right: Basket of strawberries

Divinity Fudge

2 cups (500 mL) sugar
1/2 cup (125 mL) corn syrup
1/2 cup (125 mL) water
2 stiffly beaten egg whites
Vanilla or almond flavouring
Cherries or nuts

Combine sugar, corn syrup, and
water and cook until hardball stage.
Pour over egg whites and, using an
egg beater, beat until thick. Continue beating with a spoon until
mixture stays in shape when
dropped from spoon. Add vanilla
and cherries or nuts. Drop onto wax
paper.

Photo: City Hall, Fredericton

56

This is a birthday favourite when served over vanilla ice cream.

Foshay Fudge Sauce

1/2 cup (125 mL) butter
2 sq unsweetened chocolate
1/8 tsp (1 mL) salt
1-1/2 cups (375 mL) sugar
1 cup (250 mL) Carnation evaporated milk
1 tsp (5 mL) vanilla

In a double boiler, heat together butter and chocolate until melted. Stir in salt and sugar in 4 or 5 portions, blending well after each addition. Stir in milk very slowly and cook sauce for 5 more minutes or until slightly thickened. Add vanilla.

Photo: Christ Church, Bloomfield Station

Dulse, an edible seaweed found on Grand Manan Island, may be served as a condiment, snack, or vegetable. It is a good source of potassium, iron, sodium, magnesium, and iodine.

Dark Harbour Dulse Bread

1/2 cup (125 mL) chopped dulse
1/2 cup (125 mL) oatmeal
1/2 cup (125 mL) boiling water
2 tsp (10 mL) sugar
2 tbsp (25 mL) yeast
1/2 cup (125 mL) warm water
4 to 5 cups (1 to 1.25 L) flour

Add chopped dulse and oatmeal to boiling water. Add 1 tsp (5 mL) sugar while stirring. Let cool. Add remaining sugar and yeast to warm water; let dissolve. Combine yeast and dulse mixtures, mixing well. Add flour until dough becomes thick. Knead well. Place dough in a bowl and let rise until double in size. Knead again. Shape loaf and let rise until double in size. Bake in a 400°F (200°C) oven for 15 minutes. Reduce temperature to 350°F (180°C) and bake for 45 more minutes or until lightly browned.

Left: Hilltop house, Woodstock
Right: Dulse drying in the sun, Dark Harbour, Grand Manan

Grammy's Brown Bread

1 pkg yeast
1/2 cup (125 mL) warm water
1 tsp (5 mL) sugar
2 cups (500 mL) water
2 cups (500 mL) rolled oats
5 tsp (25 mL) salt
1/4 cup (50 mL) bacon fat
1/3 cup (75 mL) molasses
2 cups (500 mL) cold milk
1 cup (250 mL) whole-wheat flour
1/2 cup (125 mL) shredded wheat
5 cups (1.25 L) white flour

Prepare yeast in mixture of warm water and sugar, according to package directions. Bring 2 cups (500 mL) water to a boil. Add rolled oats and salt, cooking and stirring until thick. Remove from heat and add bacon fat, molasses, milk, and yeast mixture. Add whole-wheat flour and shredded wheat. Beat for 1 minute. Add white flour 1 cup (250 mL) at a time until dough is no longer sticky. Knead until smooth and firm, about 10 minutes. Form into a ball. Grease a bowl and dough with bacon fat. Let dough rise in bowl until double in size, about 1-1/2 hours. Punch down. Form into 2 loaves and one 9-inch x 9-inch (23-cm x 23-cm) pan of rolls. Let rise again until double in size. Bake in a 350°F (180°C) oven for 45 minutes, brushing tops with butter.

Note: If desired, substitute corn-meal, wheat germ, or graham flour for shredded wheat.

Left: Child playing in daisies
Right: Linen and lace, New Brunswick Museum, Saint John

Indian Relish

15 to 20 large cucumbers
3 tbsp (50 mL) salt
2 to 3 lb (1 to 1.5 kg) onions
1/4 tsp (1 mL) ground red pepper
1 tbsp (15 mL) mustard seeds
1 tsp (5 mL) celery seeds
1/2 tsp (2 mL) turmeric
3 cups (750 mL) sugar
3 cups (750 mL) cider vinegar

Peel cucumbers and remove all seeds. Put through a food chopper, measure 7 cups (1.75 L), and sprinkle with salt. Let stand overnight, then drain. Peel onions, put through food chopper, and measure 3-1/2 cups (875 mL). Add onions, spices, sugar, and vinegar to cucumbers. Bring to a soft boil and continue cooking for 45 minutes. Let cool slightly, then pour into sterilized bottles and seal with wax. Makes about 7 pt (3.5 L).

62

Chow Chow

1/2 peck (4 kg) green tomatoes
2-1/2 lb (1.25 kg) onions
1/2 cup (125 mL) salt
4 tbsp (60 mL) mixed pickling spices
6 whole cloves
2 cups (500 mL) vinegar
2 cups (500 mL) sugar

Slice tomatoes and onions; combine. Sprinkle with salt and let stand overnight. Drain well. Tie pickling spices and cloves in a thin cotton bag. Add to tomatoes and onions and cover with vinegar. Add sugar. Bring mixture to a boil, then simmer until tomatoes and onions are transparent. Remove spice bag after desired taste is reached. Pour into sterilized jars and seal with wax.

Photo: Pickles, vinegar, and seasoning

63

Cut Spiced Herring

10 lb (5 kg) cleaned, vinegar-cured
  herring
Sliced onions
2 oz (50 g) bay leaves
3 oz (75 g) whole allspice
2 oz (50 g) mustard seeds
1 oz (25 g) black peppercorns
1 oz (25 g) red peppers
1 oz (25 g) white peppercorns
1/2 oz (15 g) whole cloves
1 oz (25 g) sugar
1 pt (500 mL) water
1 qt (1 L) vinegar

Cut herring crosswise into 1- to
1-1/2-inch (2.5- to 3.5-cm) pieces.

In a crock, layer herring alternately
with onions, bay leaves, and spices.
Dissolve sugar in water. Add vinegar
and pour over herring. Before using,
let stand in a cold place for 24
hours.

Note: After herring stands, you may
repack it in 1-pt (500-mL) or 1-qt
(1-L) jars. (Do not use rubber rings,
as vinegar causes them to deterio-
rate.) Refrigerate for up to 6 months,
adding fresh spices and a slice of
lemon.

Photo: Weir at sunset, Bay of Fundy